AYO'S **AWESOME** ADVENTURES IN

RABAT

CAPITAL OF MOROCCO

WORLD BOOK

www.worldbook.com

World Book, Inc.
180 North LaSalle Street
Suite 900
Chicago, Illinois 60601
USA

For information about other World Book publications, visit our website at www.worldbook.com or call 1-800-WORLDBK (967-5325).

For information about sales to schools and libraries, call 1-800-975-3250 (United States), or 1-800-837-5365 (Canada).

Library of Congress Cataloging-in-Publication Data for this volume has been applied for.

Ayo's Awesome Adventures
ISBN: 978-0-7166-3636-6 (set, hc.)

Ayo's Awesome Adventures in Rabat:
Capital of Morocco
ISBN: 978-0-7166-3643-4 (hc.)

Also available as:
ISBN: 978-0-7166-3654-0 (e-book)

1st printing July 2018

Staff

Writer: Nathalie Strassheim

Executive Committee

President
Jim O'Rourke

Vice President and
Editor in Chief
Paul A. Kobasa

Vice President, Finance
Donald D. Keller

Vice President, Marketing
Jean Lin

Vice President, International Sales
Maksim Rutenberg

Vice President, Technology
Jason Dole

Director, Human Resources
Bev Ecker

Editorial

Director, New Print
Tom Evans

Managing Editor, New Print
Jeff De La Rosa

Series Editor
Nathalie Strassheim

Librarian
S. Thomas Richardson

Manager, Contracts & Compliance
(Rights & Permissions)
Loranne K. Shields

Manager, Indexing Services
David Pofelski

Digital

Director, Digital Product
Development
Erika Meller

Manager, Digital Products
Jonathan Wills

Graphics and Design

Senior Art Director
Tom Evans

Senior Visual Communications
Designer
Melanie Bender

Senior Web Designer/Digital
Media Developer
Matthew Carrington

Media Researcher
Rosalia Bledsoe

Senior Cartographer
John M. Rejba

**Manufacturing/
Production**

Manufacturing Manager
Anne Fritzinger

Proofreaders
Mary Kieffer
Georgina Milsted

Contents

Introduction

Hello! Are you ready for an adventure? My name is Ayo. I'm an aardvark, an African mammal that eats ants and termites. I am also a tour guide traveling the world. I hope you

will come with me. In this book, we will visit the city of Rabat.

Rabat is in the country of Morocco. It is Morocco's capital city. Morocco is in the northwest corner of the continent of Africa. Africa is my home continent! And my name is an African word that means *joy*.

Many people in Rabat do not speak English. In fact, most of the places we will visit have names in French or Arabic. I'll slowly sound out words that are probably new and strange to you. When you tell your friends about your trip and use these new words, you will sound quite smart! Here's an example. The name of the city, Rabat, is said *rah BAHT.* That's pretty easy. Let's try another one. Some places in Rabat were built by people called Andalusians. That's a big word! It is said *AN duh LOO zhuhnz.*

We'll also talk about many things that may be new to you. If I can explain them easily, I will do so right away. If a word cannot be explained very easily, or if I use the word over and over again, I will put it in boldface. Boldface is type that **looks like this.** All boldface words will be defined in a glossary in the back of the book.

I hope someday you can travel with your family to Rabat. You can ask to see the places we visit in this book! Then you can be the tour guide for your parents and brothers and sisters.

Rabat information

- Population: 577,827
- Founded: In the 1100's
- Influences: People from many places have lived in Rabat. You can see evidence of Roman, Muslim, Spanish, and French culture.

Morocco information

- Climate: Mild on the coast and hot inland, with rainy and dry seasons
- Money: Moroccan dirham. One hundred centimes equal one dirham.
- Flag: Officially adopted in 1915. It features a five-pointed green star on a red background.

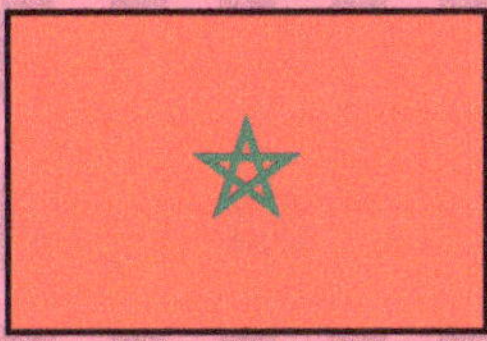

flag of Morocco

Walls and gates

I am excited to show you around Rabat! Let's begin with the city's famous walls. They stretch for miles or kilometers through Rabat. Who would build such walls?

The **Andalusians** built one of the most famous. The Andalusian Wall separates part of Rabat called the **medina** from the rest of the city. It was built during the 1600's.

The city's main wall was built even earlier, in the 1100's. It was built under the rule of a man named Abu Yusuf Ya`qub al-Mansour. (We can call him Yacoub el Mansour.) His name means Yacoub the Victorious. He won battles and wanted to build a great capital city. He built about 3 miles (5 kilometers) of walls! His enemies would not be able to jump over walls that are up to 33 feet (10 meters) tall. They also could not break through walls 8 feet (2.5 meters) thick.

What are the walls made of?

- Stones
- Earth
- Ocher *(OH kuhr)* plaster. Ocher is a type of brownish-red earth ground into a powder.
- Cement. Cement is a fine gray powder mixed with other things to make a hard material.

Who are the Andalusians?

The Andalusians who settled in Rabat were **Muslims** from Spain. They were *banished* (sent away) from Spain in the early 1600's. Many became pirates and captured trading ships on the Atlantic Ocean.

A "wall" of water

Rabat is protected on two sides by water. The Atlantic Ocean is on the northwest side. A river called the Bou Regreg is on the northeast side. The Bou Regreg flows into the Atlantic Ocean.

Yacoub's wall has several gates. They include Bab el Had, Bab el Alou, and Bab Zaer. (*Bab* is an Arabic word for *gate.*) The gate I want to show you is Bab er Rouah. Some people call it Gate of the Winds. It faces west, the direction from which many ocean winds blow. Those arch shapes around the door are made up of carved flowers and plants all twisted

together, called *arabesques (AR uh BEHSKS)*. You can see them up close.

Let's go inside. This gate is huge! Inside the gate building, there is enough space for four rooms with high, round ceilings called *domes*. Today, these rooms are used as galleries, places where people show art and other important things.

Kasbah of the Oudaïas

Let's explore one of the oldest places in Rabat, the **Kasbah** of the Oudaïas *(oo DAY uh)*. A family of rulers settled here and built a fortress—with walls! Yacoub the Victorious built Bab Oudaïa, the huge gate we're standing in front of.

Things look very different inside the kasbah walls. The side streets and alleys are narrow. The houses are white and blue. Guess who built most of these houses—the **Andalusians!**

At the end of Rue Jamaa, French for Street of the **Mosque,** we'll find the semaphore platform. It looks out over the river and the Atlantic Ocean. Hundreds of years ago, people could stand here to signal to pirate ships. They used semaphore, a method of signaling with flags.

Bab Oudaïa

The stone carvings over the gate have the same pattern as on Hassan Tower (page 36). It is called *darj w ktaf* and looks a little like tulips.

darj w ktaf

No one signals to pirate ships from here anymore, and I'm too short anyway. No one could see me waving flags! But there is a carpet workshop. We can watch people weave carpets on traditional looms operated by hand, rather than modern machinery.

Andalusian Gardens

Wow, it can get hot during the day! Now you know why aardvarks like to sleep when the sun is out and find food at night. But we can take a break in the Andalusian Gardens. They are hidden behind walls at one end of the **Kasbah** of the Oudaïas.

It's so green and colorful here with the fruit trees and flowering shrubs. A waterwheel called a *noria* moves water through the flower beds. Everything looks a little tangled and wild when it spills out of the beds. When the hibiscus and morning glories bloom, it smells wonderful here!

How do we get in? The most delicious way is through the Café Maure. Many **Rabatis** and visitors like us sit on the *terrace*, or open sitting area. Make sure you try the mint tea and cornes de gazelle *(kawrn duh guh ZEHL)*. These pastries are filled with almond paste, a local specialty. (I would prefer termites.) When we're done, we can slip through the doorway into the gardens.

Café Maure and cornes de gazelle (lower left)

Who built the
Andalusian Gardens?

Not the **Andalusians!**
A French scholar
named Prosper Ricard
designed the gardens
in the early 1900's.

What grows here?
• Date palms
• Lemon, banana,
  and orange trees
• Bougainvillea
• Herbs
• Red hibiscus
• Morning glories

Medina

Across the street from the **kasbah** is Rabat's **medina.** Let's explore the narrow streets and traditional markets. But first, we will stop at the Artisanal Center. Look at all the interesting things people in Rabat make! The traditional shoes don't fit aardvarks, but you might like a pair. I also see mosaics, pottery, and painted wood.

Wait, you don't like it when your parents make you go shopping with them? This is different—really. Follow me across the street. I like this outdoor market, the one without cars. It's called the Rue des Consuls *(roo day kon SOOL).* It has an arched plexiglass roof with neat black patterns. Plexiglass looks like glass, but it is really a kind of plastic. We can visit shop after shop selling the same things as the Artisanal Center. Do you want to pay less for that leather bag? You can *haggle—* that is, you can bargain with the seller to get a lower price.

Saving the medina

Over the years, many North African medinas were knocked down. New buildings took their place. But Rabat's medina got lucky. Marshal Hubert Lyautey, a French official, thought the medina should be preserved as part of Moroccan culture. He ordered that new buildings had to be located south of the Andalusian Wall, away from the medina.

Rue des Consuls

At this corner, we turn right and join the crowd in the Souk es Sebbat. A roof covers this **souk,** or outdoor street market. The roof is made of grasslike plants called *rushes.* We keep bumping into tourists on this street. They are shopping for jewelry, colorful fabric, and leather goods.

Have you noticed how the shops are changing? The street name changed, too. We are now walking down the Rue Souïka, which means *Little Souk Street.* Not as many tourists are with us, because the shops here sell everyday items, such as spices, modern shoes, and food.

On Avenue Mohammed V, we find restaurants, cafes, and street vendors. Mmmmm, something smells good. Is it pastries dripping with syrup? Or freshly squeezed sugar cane juice? Have you tried babouche *(bah BOOSH)?* It's a specialty— small snails in spicy soup.

At a café, we can order a tagine *(tuh ZHEEN).* It is both a meal and the name of the dish it is cooked in. See how the cover is wide at the bottom and rises to a small hole? Steam turns into water on the inside and runs back into the food, so our food doesn't dry out! We can order a tagine with meat, vegetables, or both. But no termite tagines.

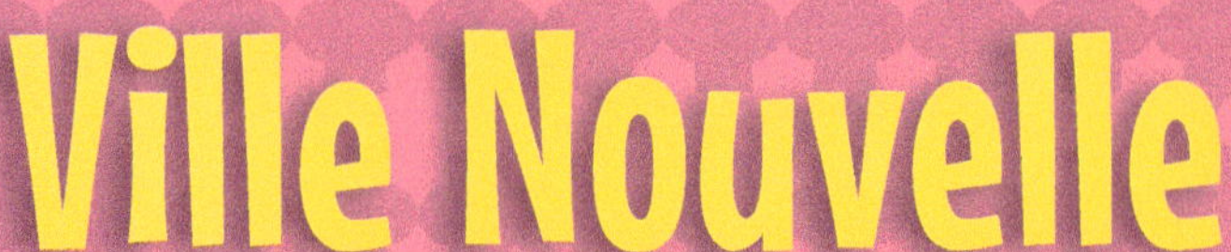

Ville Nouvelle

After our snack, let's follow Avenue Mohammed V south through the Andalusian Wall. We'll explore the **ville nouvelle** *(VEEL noo VEHL)*. Everything seems different! The streets are wider, the buildings are newer, and there are open parks. A large park on our left is Jardin Nouzhat Hassan *(zhawr DAHN noo ZHAHT hah SAHN)*. We can stroll through shady paths and rest on benches beneath large trees. The French built the park in the early 1900's.

In fact, the French built a lot of what you see on the south side of the Andalusian Wall. In 1912, the French took control of Morocco. (At the time, European countries were still trying to control parts of Africa.) Marshal Lyautey ordered the construction of the ville nouvelle within Yacoub el Mansour's wall, south of the medina.

Another Andalusian Garden was built in the early 2000's, in the middle of the Jardin d'Essais Botaniques *(zhawr DAHN dess AY boh tan EEK)*, a garden where scientists experiment with growing plants. This Andalusian Garden has walls, too! Here, we will find out what Muslims in Spain hundreds of years ago liked to plant and how they watered their gardens. (Spain is also a dry place.)

After our tour of the Jardin d'Essais Botaniques, let's return to the center of the **ville nouvelle.** Avenue Mohammed V seems to run right into the grand Assouna **Mosque** before curving around it. Avenue Yacoub al Mansour curves around the other side and runs south to Bab Zaer and Chellah.

If we head down the Avenue Bab Soufara, we'll come to a big open space called a *méchouar (may koo AHR).* That's another way of saying *gathering place.*

We can walk across the méchouar from the Ahl Fas Mosque to the Dar El-Makhzen. This is the official royal residence. We aren't allowed very close, but we might be able to see the beautiful colors on the gate. Some guards wear red and white uniforms. They'll tell us to move along if we stay too long! Not even aardvarks may tour the large group of buildings where many officials work and, sometimes, the king and his family live. I have heard that nearly 2,000 people live and work behind that gate.

Morocco has had a king since it gained independence from France in 1956. The first king after independence was Mohammed V. Many things in Rabat are named after him and his son, King Hassan II.

Dar El-Makhzen

Bank Al-Maghrib Museum

Do you like looking at the coins in your pocket? (I don't have any pockets. I'm an aardvark, not a kangaroo!) I do enjoy organizing my coins by year and whether there are people or buildings on them. Rabat has the perfect place to go to see lots of coins. Right in the **ville nouvelle,** the Bank Al-Maghrib has a museum just for kids like us—the Bank Al-Maghrib Museum. There are about 1,200 coins here.

Look at some of these really old coins! They are from a time long ago, when ancient Greece was an important civilization. This coin has an owl on one side. It is from Athens, a powerful city-state. Owl coins were one of the first important *trading currencies*, which is the kind of money people use to buy things.

There are even coins from Carthage and Rome. For many years, Morocco was part of the Carthaginian empire, which stretched across northern Africa. We can see a coin that King Juba II, a local ruler, had made when he got married. It's called a golden aureus. And then there is a Roman coin with the first emperor's name stamped on it: Augustus.

Archaeological Museum

In the **ville nouvelle,** we can visit the four rooms of the Archaeological Museum. *Archaeology* is the study of things left behind by people long ago.

In the first room, we can see a map of recent archaeological digs. On the floor is a *mosaic*, a picture made of tiny colored tiles. It's from Volubilis, an ancient Roman town east of Rabat. The picture on the facing page shows what Volubilis looks like now. Do you see a mosaic?

More **artifacts** from Volubilis are in the Salle des Bronzes *(sahl day BRONZ),* which is how French people say *room of bronzes.* Do you think people in Volubilis made bronze statues of aardvarks? No, I don't either. Some famous things to see:

• *Ephebe Crowned with Ivy,* a statue of a young soldier.

• The *Dog of Volubilis (below).* Archaeologists think this dog statue was used to decorate a public bath.

In the third room, we can look at axes, arrowheads, swords, and pottery from thousands of years ago. They help us imagine life before electricity and machines.

The fourth room tells us more about Chellah *(SHEHL uh),* a site we will visit. Archaeologists have found Roman things there, such as oil lamps. Christians lived in Chellah, too, and left behind an altar and a small ivory statue of the Good Shepherd.

Long ago Romans controlled the area where Rabat is today.
You know, aardvarks really like to dig, too.

Chellah

Now let's visit the place where the Chellah **artifacts** in the Archaeological Museum were found. First, we go through Bab Zaer, another gate in the walls built by Yacoub the Victorious. Then we'll walk down a path to a gate in the walls around Chellah. From a viewing platform, we can look out over the Bou Regreg river valley. Do you see how the land *slopes*, or goes down, toward the river? Romans built a town here because it was easy to get to the river.

The ancient Romans called their town Sala Colonia. What will we find when we walk through its ruins?
- The Temple of Jupiter, which honored an important Roman god.
- What's left of a triumphal arch (a large stone monument) and the forum, a place where people gathered.
- The Craftsmen's Quarter, where people who made things lived and kept their shops.

We can still see parts of the road to the river and even some of the port, down at the river's edge. (Most of the port has been buried in sand.) The Romans abandoned Sala Colonia almost a thousand years ago. They moved across the river and started the city now known as Salé.

The ruler Abou el Hassan built Chellah's walls, including 20 towers and the gate. He is buried in the necropolis, where we're headed next.

Guess what happened in 1755—an earthquake struck! Since the earthquake, flowers, brambles, and trees have grown around the ruined buildings. Birds called *storks* have taken over the trees and the **minaret!** But I haven't seen any aardvarks snuffling in the bushes.

After Sala Colonia, we can visit a necropolis, which is a fancy word meaning *city of the dead*. That sounds scary, but it is really just a cemetery. This one is actually very beautiful and peaceful. About 100 years after the Romans left Sala Colonia, a ruler named Abou Youssef decided this place would be just right for his wife's grave and a **mosque.** He and the rulers who followed built several tombs; a zaouia *(zhah oo OY ah),* a place to study religion; and a minaret. We can see the outline of the zaouia's pool and the columns that used to stand around it.

Outside the cemetery, we will find a spring-fed pool inside some low buildings. It is called the Bassin aux Anguilles *(BASS uh ohz ahn GEE).* Special eels live in the pools. Many **Rabatis** come here to feed boiled eggs to them. Rabatis think this will bring good luck.

Mosques of Rabat

When we walk through the streets, we see a lot of **mosques.** Many people in Morocco are **Muslims.** I think we should find some of the most famous mosques because they can be beautiful buildings.

Did you see the El Atika Mosque when you were in the **kasbah?** The oldest in Rabat, it was built in 1150. In the 1700's, the pirate Ahmed el Inlisi gave money to rebuild the mosque. (*El inlisi* means *the Englishman*.)

When we walk through the **medina's** Souk es Sebbat, we can admire the Grand Mosque. Look up at its **minaret**—look way up because it is 109 feet (33 meters) tall! Its **zellij** decoration was only finished in 1939! Other parts were rebuilt over the centuries.

In the **ville nouvelle,** we will find the Assouna Mosque at one end of the wide Avenue Mohammed V. It looks old, doesn't it? In the 1960's, the builders made it in the traditional North African style called Maghrebi. It overlooks the length of the avenue named after King Mohammed V.

minaret of
Assouna Mosque

If you are not
a Muslim, you
cannot go into
a mosque. But
we can look at
the outside.

Mohammed V Mausoleum

Look up and around! The ceiling is a dome with 12 sides. It has been carved and covered with very thin sheets of gold, called *gold leaf*. We can see light coming through many stained-glass windows. They were made in France. The walls are covered in **zellij**.

We have visited many very old places in Rabat. Let's see something a little newer. We'll start at a large, open area called Yacoub el Mansour Square. On one side sits the Mausoleum of Mohammed V. A mausoleum *(MAW suh LEE uhm)* is a tomb. King Hassan II, who was alive about 60 years ago, built it to honor his father, King Mohammed V.

To get into the mausoleum, we have to go through wrought-iron gates and up many stairs. Inside, we have to stay on a balcony.

The balcony goes around the room where the bodies of King Mohammed V and his sons King Hassan II and Prince Moulay Abdallah rest in three sarcophaguses. A sarcophagus *(sahr KOF uh guhs)* is a container for a dead body. King Mohammed's is the biggest one, in the middle of the room. It was made from a single block of white marble.

Hassan Tower and Mosque

All those posts on Yacoub el Mansour Square look like a strange kind of forest, don't they? These columns are the remains of what was meant to be one of the world's largest **mosques.** When Yacoub the Victorious was building his walls, he was also planning an enormous mosque. He wanted all the soldiers in his army to pray together. That would have meant nearly 40,000 people in one place!

Hassan Tower is the **minaret** of Yacoub's unfinished mosque. The top is 144 feet (44 meters) above aardvark height—only half as tall as Yacoub planned! I wish we could go inside, but visitors aren't allowed. I can *tell* you what's inside. Imagine going up a ramp instead of stairs to reach each level. (There are six levels.) The ramp is genius! Builders could take materials to higher levels more easily than with stairs.

What happened to the mosque?

Yacoub didn't live long enough to finish his mosque. He died in 1199, and building work stopped. Only a hall with a cedar roof was finished, along with some columns to support it. But then in 1755, a huge earthquake destroyed the building. Only about 200 partial columns remain. That's what we see today.

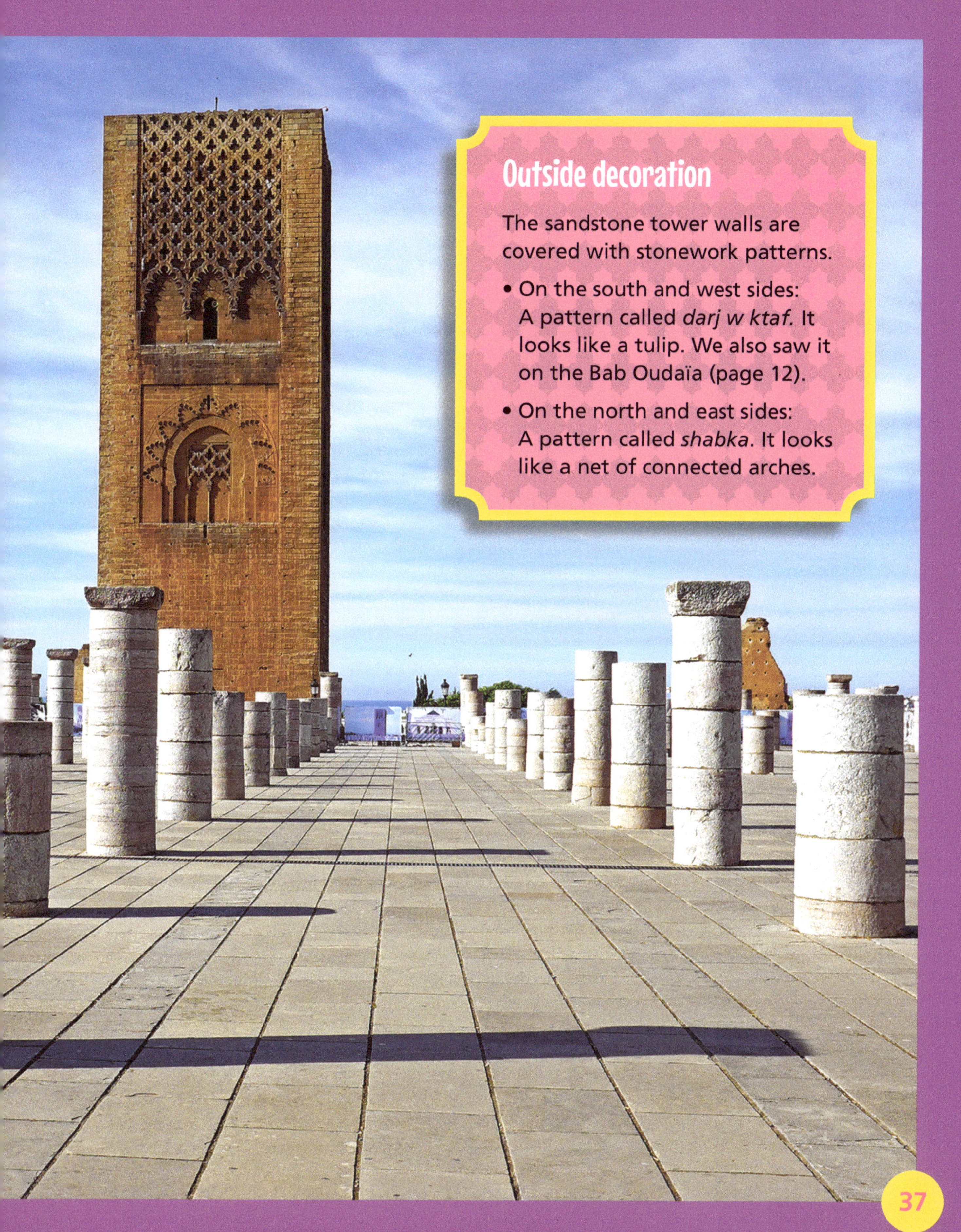

Outside decoration

The sandstone tower walls are covered with stonework patterns.

- On the south and west sides: A pattern called *darj w ktaf.* It looks like a tulip. We also saw it on the Bab Oudaïa (page 12).

- On the north and east sides: A pattern called *shabka.* It looks like a net of connected arches.

Salé

I've been wondering about Rabat's sister city, Salé *(sah LAY)*. We saw it across the river when sipping mint tea at the Café Maure. I think we should cross the river and find out more about it.

Salé is known for the traditional markets in its **medina.** The easiest way to get in is through the Bab Mrisa. The name means *Gate of the Sea*.

If we follow the wall to our left after going through Bab Mrisa, we will come to a street that sounds yummy—Rue Bab el Khebaz (Street of the Bakers' Gate). This street leads to a covered market called a *kissaria* and other **souks.** Souk el Ghezel sells things made from wool. In the Souk el Kebir, the grand souk, we'll find things made from wood, leather, and iron, plus carpets. I hope you like wandering among the different stalls as much as I do. Every time I come here, I discover something else I have never seen before.

When the walls
and gates of Salé were
built in the 1200's,
a part of the river
ran right into town.
Ships could sail into
the town! Bab Mrisa
opens to a height of
36 feet (11 meters)
to let ships' masts
through. But now it is
dry land by Bab Mrisa.

While we're in Salé, we should visit the medersa *(muh DAIR suh),* a school where people study the religion of Islam. It is no longer a school, and the government has fixed it up into a historical attraction.

Inside the medersa, built in the early 1300's, decorated walls surround a courtyard. The decorations are amazing! It seems like every flat surface is covered with **zellij** or carved cedar woodwork. On the upper floors, we can peek inside the small rooms. Then we can climb stairs to the roof! From the roof, we can look across the river to see such landmarks as the **kasbah** and Hassan Tower.

Before we head back to Rabat, let's go to the Magic Park. We can bang around in bumper cars or swoop around in carnival rides with names such as Dragon Adventures or Magic Twister. Magic Park is down by the Bou Regreg.

There are three ways to get to Salé.

(1) Take the ferry. Boats leave when they are full.

(2) Ride the air-conditioned tram across the bridge. It drops you off right at the Bab Mrisa.

(3) Take a taxi.

Rabat Zoo

Finally, one of my favorite places in any city—the zoo! We will meet nearly 130 kinds of animals. (But, I'm sad to say, no other aardvarks.)

The name of the zoo is Jardin Zoologique de Rabat (*zhar DAN zoh oh loh ZHEEK duh ruh BAHT*). This zoo's specialty is animals of Africa, especially Morocco and grasslands of the savanna.

I like seeing animals in the kind of ecosystem they are used to. As you may already have learned in school, an ecosystem is made up of a group of living things, the place where they live, and the relationship between the living things and the place. Animals here live in five different kinds of ecosystems. As we walk through the zoo, we will visit these areas and might meet these friends:

Mountains – Atlas lion, Barbary macaque, Barbary sheep, Barbary ground squirrel

Savanna – white rhinoceros, meerkat, giraffe, eland

Desert – addax, fennec fox, tortoise, ostrich

Wetlands – African buffalo, white pelican, hippopotamus, flamingo

Tropical forest – serval, lemur, python, ibis

If we get hungry, let's stop at one of the restaurants. The most interesting one has a view over the savanna habitat. I hope they have termites on toast, or ants à la mode!

Atlas
lions
lemur
fennec foxes
addaxes

Bab er Rouah
Ville Nouvelle
Medina
Hassan Tower and Mosque

Andalusian Gardens
Thanks for exploring Rabat with me. I hope to see you soon!
Ayo

Glossary

Andalusians *(AN duh LOO zhuhnz)* Muslims who were banished from Spain. They settled in northern Africa.

artifact *(AHR tuh fakt)* Object made by human hands

kasbah *(KAHZ bah)* Fortress in a North African city

medina *(muh DEE nuh)* The native Arab area of a city in North Africa

minaret *(MIHN uh REHT)* A tall, usually slender, tower attached to a mosque

mosque *(mosk)* Muslim house of worship

Muslim *(MUHZ luhm)* A follower of the religion of Islam

Rabati *(ruh BAH tee)* A person who lives in Rabat

souk *(sook)* Outdoor street market

ville nouvelle *(VEEL noo VEHL)* The new area of a city

zellij *(ZEHL eezh)* Small, colored tiles arranged in patterns

Acknowledgments

Cover © Denis Kabanov, Shutterstock
Ayo artwork by Matthew Carrington

4-7   © Shutterstock
8-9   © Alamy Images
10-11 © Leonid Andronov, Shutterstock; © Shutterstock
12-13 © Alamy Images; © Dreamstime; © Patricia Hofmeester, Shutterstock
14-15 © Hemis/Alamy Images; © Foodpictures/Shutterstock; © Sarah Lois, Shutterstock
16-17 © John Kellerman, Alamy Images
18-19 © Patricia Hofmeester, Shutterstock; © Rafal Cichawa, Shutterstock; © Margouillat Photos/iStockphoto
20-21 Etotheraf (licensed under CC BY-SA 4.0)
22-25 © Shutterstock
26-27 © Shutterstock; Maxim Massalitin (licensed under CC BY-SA 2.0)
28-31 © Shutterstock
32-33 © Hemis/Alamy Images
34-35 © Saiko3p/Shutterstock; Amine Bahdod (licensed under CC BY-SA 4.0)
36-37 © Steve Photography, Shutterstock
38-39 © Dreamstime; © Shutterstock
40-41 © Alamy Images; © Alex7370/Shutterstock
42-43 © Alamy Images; © Dave Watts, Alamy Images; © Pdxnative/Dreamstime

Index

For further reading

Books

DK Publishing, *DK Eyewitness Travel Guide: Morocco.* DK Publishing: New York, 2010.

French, Carol. *National Geographic Traveler: Morocco.* National Geographic Society: Washington, DC, 2011.

Simmons, Walter. *Morocco.* Bellwether Media: Minnetonka, MN, 2012.

Websites

Three different guides to visiting Rabat

http://www.frommers.com/destinations/rabat

https://www.lonelyplanet.com/morocco/rabat

http://www.morocco.com/rabat-sale-zemmour-zaer/rabat/